AWESOME
ATVs

by Tori Kosara

SCHOLASTIC INC.

P9-DTA-501

ATVs

(All-terrain vehicles) are supercool machines that can tackle any kind of ground—from sticky mud to jagged rock. But they can do a whole lot more than just take drivers for a fun trip.

Ride on to find out about all the incredible things these marvelous machines can do.

ATVs were invented in Japan during the twentieth century. Farmers had a tough time driving over muddy mountainous land, so they designed a vehicle that could easily drive through mud and other tricky surfaces.

The first ATV was made with three wheels, but now these machines can have up to eight wheels. ATVs have handlebars, like motorcycles, which the driver uses to steer, and powerful engines that help drive over rough ground.

They might not be made for speed, but riders enjoy racing their ATVs. A popular sport, ATV races are very exciting. Riders splash through puddles and crawl over sharp rocks to make it to the finish line.

he average ATV can reach speeds of about 50 mph (80.5 kph). So what's the fastest vehicle on the trail? Speeds can vary, but some riders think the 2008 Polaris Outlaw 525 IRS is the fastest because it can reach 50 mph (80.5 kph) in just over five seconds!

Sport ATVs are made to go fast! Riders enjoy taking these vehicles out for a spin on trails, tracks, and sand dunes—where they can speed up quickly.

ATV riders who want to go for a comfortable drive enjoy going out in side-by-sides. This special type of ATV has more than one seat so that more passengers can hit the trails. Side-by-sides can have up to six seats and include seat belts. But they can still move pretty fast—hitting speeds of 60 mph (96.6 kph).

Not just for fun, ATVs can also be used for hard work. Riders can use their machines to haul heavy loads. How much weight the ATV can pull depends on its size, but these

powerful vehicles have been known to pull over 800 pounds (363 kilograms)—that's almost three times the weight of a giant panda!

All-Terrain Vehicles are not only for land use. Amphibious ATVs can go in the water! They are used for fun, like fishing, and for work during natural disasters, like floods.

When things get hot, ATVs are good to have around! Firefighters can count on ATVs to take them over land or water

to get to an emergency quickly. This different kind of fire truck can carry lots of fire equipment and up to six firefighters.

Two of the most famous ATVs are the Mars Rovers. These Rovers were built to explore Mars by moving on their own across the surface and gathering rocks and soil. One of the Rovers, named *Curiosity*, is currently on a mission on Mars searching for evidence of life on the Red Planet.

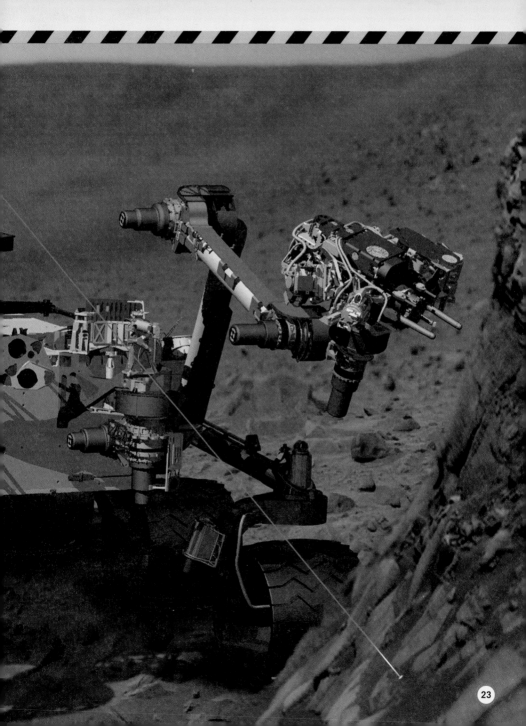

All-Terrain Vehicles drive through slippery snow with ease, and that makes them great for plowing. Riders can attach a special plow to the front of their machines that will let them push snow out of the way and clear a safe path even on the slickest of surfaces.

Did you know that ATVs can be spies? The military relies on these magnificent machines to go on missions. This ATV can travel over any kind of land without a driver. It is set up

with special equipment that helps it find its way and get the information it needs in order to act as an amazing spy!

The military also uses ATVs to haul stuff because they can carry lots of heavy and important gear. These reliable vehicles can

carry people and supplies over dangerous land and water just about anywhere in the world.

ATVs are extremely useful. Drivers can attach special parts to their machines to help them do lots of things, like mow a lawn, plow a field, and even act as a crane.

ATVs are amazing vehicles that are built for fun and hard work. What kinds of cool things do you think ATVs will do next?

SCHOLASTIC INC.

AMAZING MOTORCYCLES

BY TORI KOSARA

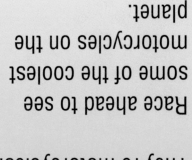

MOTORCYCLES

They may look like bicycles, but these superpowered bikes are superfast—racing at speeds that can top that of most cars. They can jump, race, and even perform surprising stunts. They're motorcycles!

Race ahead to see some of the coolest motorcycles on the planet.

Motorcycles are big bikes with two wheels and no pedals. They are powered by engines, so they can zoom around much faster than bicycles.

Not all motorcycles
have just two
wheels. Some
have three, just like
a tricycle. Most of
these get the third
wheel from a sidecar.
A sidecar is a seat
that is hitched to
the motorcycle.
Passengers, or
even pets, can
ride in a sidecar.

Daimler's wooden
motorcycle

The first ever motorcycle is believed to have been built in 1885—and was made mostly of wood! It didn't look much like modern-day motorcycles. The bike had two wheels called stabilizers that look like the training wheels on a bicycle.

Motorcycles can go fast—really fast! So far, the fastest motorcycle was recorded at a speed of 376 mph (605 kph). A new motorcycle called the Jet Reaction uses the

engine from a helicopter to give the bike a boost. It's thought that this motorcycle will be able to reach speeds of over 400 mph (644 kph)—that's almost as fast as a plane!

The average motorcycle weighs about 500 pounds (227 kilograms). But this monster motorcycle is one of the biggest ridable bikes in the world. It weighs over 6,500 pounds (2,948

kilograms), and is 15 feet (4.6 meters) high and 25 feet (7.6 meters) long! It may weigh even more than the average hippo, but this monstrous machine can still do jumps.

Not all motorcycles are massive. Some are super small. One of the world's tiniest ridable motorcycles weighs just over

2 pounds (0.9 kilograms), and is only 3.14 inches (8 centimeters) long. This tiny bike, known as Smalltoe, has a top speed of 1.24 mph (1.99 kph).

Sportbikes are a special kind of motorcycle that are made for speed, swift turning around tricky corners, and quick stopping on the road. Some riders who like to go really fast enjoy taking sportbikes for a spin. But most sportbike riders use these special motorcycles for races.

The most popular kind of motorcycle in the United States is known as a cruiser. This type of bike is great for riding long distances. Some of the best-known cruisers

are Harley-Davidson motorcycles. It's said that the first Harley-Davidson, which was built in 1903, used a tomato can as part of the engine— but no one knows for sure.

Not all motorcycles are made for the road. Off-road motorcycles, also called dirt bikes, are made to hit the trail. These bikes have special tires that help them climb tough rocks, clear massive jumps, and speed across almost any kind of surface— even slippery sand!

Motorcycles are for kids, too! Riders who aren't old enough to take their bikes out on the road can enjoy taking safer

two-wheelers out on special courses or tracks with an adult. They can even participate in races!

Monster motorcycles aren't the only kind on the road. Scooters are smaller versions of motorcycles. The biggest difference is that they are built for shorter distances, and they don't go as fast as more massive motorbikes. The average scooter clocks in at speeds of up to 100 mph (161 kph).

Stunt riding is for highly skilled motorcyclists who can do more than just speed along the road. Some of their tricks include jumps, wheelies, and stoppies, which means that the motorcycle rolls only on the front wheel. Some stunt riders even do acrobatic moves like handstands on their bikes. But these tricks can be seriously dangerous, so only the most experienced should try stunt riding.

Since motorcycles are so fast, lots of riders enjoy racing on their bikes. One supercool sport is called motocross. Riders race their specially made motorbikes across tracks or on outdoor courses at top speed. Many of the courses include challenging surfaces or tricky hills.

B
ecause motorcycles use lots of gas when they're being pushed to reach superspeeds, new models are being made that use

electricity instead. Electric motorcycles do not need gas to run because they are powered by rechargeable electric batteries.

Motorcycles are cool to watch and fun to ride. What kinds of bikes do you think will speed into the future?